ROBERT WEREWOLF
A PLAY
Stan Cullimore

Illustrated by Bob Doucet

First Flight

Titles in First Flight

Phantom Striker
Pest Control
Shark's Fin Island
Scary!
Ping Pong with King Kong
The Fame Game
Awesome Animals
Big, Fast Rides

Car Boot Genie
Monster Cards
Ssh! My Family are Spies
Ghost Dog Mystery
Chip Boy
Sky Bikers
Surfing Three-Sixty
Something in the Kitchen
The Ghost in the Art Room
Robert and the Werewolf
The Biggest Lies Ever
Mad about Money

Badger Publishing Limited
Oldmedow Road, Hardwick Industrial Estate,
King's Lynn PE30 4JJ
Telephone: 01438 791037
www.badgerlearning.co.uk

2 4 6 8 10 9 7 5 3 1

Robert and the Werewolf   ISBN 978 1 84424 844 5

First edition 2006
This second edition 2013

Text © Stan Cullimore 2006
Complete work © Badger Publishing Limited 2006

All rights reserved. No part of this publication may be reproduced, stored in any form or by any means mechanical, electronic, recording or otherwise without the prior permission of the publisher.

The right of Stan Cullimore to be identified as author of this Work has been asserted by him in accordance with the Copyright, Designs and Patents Act 1988.

Series Editor: Jonny Zucker
Publisher: David Jamieson
Commissioning Editor: Carrie Lewis
Editor: Paul Martin
Design: Fiona Grant
Illustration: Bob Doucet

ROBERT AND THE WEREWOLF
A PLAY
Stan Cullimore

Contents

Characters **4**

Act 1 **6**

Act 2 **12**

Act 3 **20**

Act 4 **26**

Badger
LEARNING

Characters

Robert – the hero of the play

Sarah – Robert's little sister

Dad – Robert and Sarah's dad

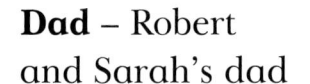

Wolf – We don't know who, or what, the wolf is…

Narrator – the person who tells you what is going on

Act 1

Narrator – Robert is on holiday with his dad and little sister, Sarah. They are in a farmhouse in Wales.

Dad – Come on, you two.

Sarah – My legs are tired.

Narrator – They are out for a walk in the hills.

Robert – Hey, Dad. Was it true what it said in that book?

Dad – Which book?

Robert – The book back at the farmhouse. It said there used to be lots of wolves in Wales.

Narrator – Dad pulled a face.

Dad – Robert! I don't want to talk about wolves! You'll frighten your sister. Now come on, Sarah – we can't sit down here.

Sarah – Why not?

Dad – Because it's starting to get dark. We have to get back to the farmhouse before the sun sets.

Robert – Why, Dad? In case a wolf gets us? Ha, ha.

Sarah – A wolf?

Dad – That's not funny, Robert! Now hurry up. It really is getting dark now.

Sarah – My legs are really tired.

Narrator – Just then, Dad fell to the ground.

Dad – (*growls*) Grrrrr.

Narrator – He turned away so that the children couldn't see his face.

Robert – What's wrong, Dad?

Dad – It's… my leg!

Robert – What about your leg?

Sarah – Does it hurt? Let me see.

Dad – (*howls*) No-o-o-o-o-o-!

Narrator – Still keeping his face hidden from the children, Dad pulled himself behind a big rock.

Dad – I must have hurt it when I fell.

Robert – What can we do to help, Dad?

Dad – Just don't come too close!

Sarah – Why not?

Dad – (*growls*) Grrrr… I just need to rest for a minute and then I will be okay. (*growls*) Grrr… Now, listen to me – both of you. You must go back to the farmhouse and wait for me there.

Robert – Are you sure, Dad?

Dad – Yes! Robert, you look after your sister. Sarah, do what Robert says. And both of you – make sure you get home before it gets dark.

Narrator – So the two children set off towards the farmhouse. After a few minutes, Robert heard a sound. He turned round.

Robert – (*gasps*)

Sarah – Robert, what is it? What can you hear?

Robert – No, it's nothing. Let's just keep moving.

Narrator – But Robert was lying. He had seen something. A pair of yellow eyes. Staring at them out of the dark…

Act 2

Wolf – (*howls*) HOOWL!

Robert – Come on, Sarah. Let's do what Dad said. Keep moving and don't look back.

Sarah – (*scared*) Okay.

Narrator – Robert looked back. The eyes had gone.

Robert – That's better.

Sarah – What is?

Robert – Nothing.

Narrator – Robert held on to Sarah's hand and started to walk a little quicker.

Robert – Here we go.

Wolf – (*deep breathing*)

Sarah – Wait! Did you hear that, Robert?

Robert – (*gulps*) No, I didn't hear anything.

Narrator – But Robert was lying again. He had heard a noise. And now it sounded like something was running behind them.

Sarah – Robert, I'm scared.

Robert – Well, don't be scared. I've had an idea.

Sarah – What?

Wolf – (*more deep breathing*)

Robert – Let's have a race back to the farmhouse.

Sarah – OK.

Narrator – They both started to run.

Sarah – You're too fast. I can't keep up!

Robert – We can't stop now!

Sarah – Why not?

Narrator – Robert could hear the sound of running. It was getting closer.

Wolf – (*growls*)

Robert – Because Dad told us not to.

Narrator – Robert looked back. In the darkness, he could see the eyes again. They were getting closer.

Sarah – Ow!

Narrator – Sarah had tripped over a rock.

Sarah – (*cries*) I want Daddy.

Robert – Well, you can't have him, he's not here.

Narrator – Robert listened. The sound of running had stopped.

Wolf – (*deep breathing*)

Narrator – Now Robert could hear the sound of breathing. It was very close.

Robert – Come on, we're very close to the farmhouse now, Sarah.

Sarah – I can't run any more.

Robert – Well, then I'll give you a piggyback.

Narrator – Sarah jumped up onto Robert's back.

Sarah – I'm scared!

Narrator – Robert ran all the way to the front door of the farmhouse.

Robert – Go inside quickly. There's nothing to be scared of.

Narrator – When they got inside, Robert locked the door.

Robert – (*sighs*) Now we're safe.

Sarah – What do you mean, Robert?

Robert – Nothing, I was just joking.

Wolf – (*howls*)

Act 3

Sarah – Robert, when is Dad coming home?

Robert – I don't know. But I hope he's okay.

Narrator – Robert heard a noise outside the door. He turned the light off.

Wolf – (*sniffs and grunts*)

Sarah – What are you doing, Robert?

Wolf – (*more sniffs and grunts*)

Robert – Er… I want to see if Dad is outside.

Sarah – Well, I'm going to watch TV.

Narrator – Sarah went to the living room at the back of the house. Robert looked out of the window.

Robert – Oh, no.

Narrator – He could see a large shape moving outside.

Robert – That does NOT look like Dad. (*gulp*) That looks like a wolf!

Wolf – (*growls*)

Narrator The shape moved away.

Robert – Now where has it gone?

Wolf – (*howls*)

Robert – Oh, no. It's gone round the back of the house. (*shouts*) Sarah, watch out!

Narrator – Robert ran into the living room.

Sarah – Are you coming to watch TV with me, Robert?

Robert – No, you can't watch TV, Sarah. You have to go upstairs.

Sarah – But I want to watch TV. I don't want to go upstairs.

Robert – (*shouts*) You HAVE to!

Narrator – Robert grabbed hold of his little sister.

Robert – Come on!

Sarah – Robert, let go.

Robert – I can't. We have to get upstairs – and fast!

Sarah – But why?

Wolf – (*howls*)

Sarah – (*scared*) Robert, that really sounds like a wolf.

Robert – I know. That's why we have to get upstairs. Come on.

Narrator – Robert took Sarah upstairs. He did not see the curtains moving in the wind.

Robert – I think we should get into the bathroom, Sarah.

Sarah – Why? I don't need to go to the bathroom.

Robert – I know. But we can lock the door.

Narrator – They both went into the bathroom.

Sarah – Robert. Should we lock the window in the living room?

Robert – The window in the living room?

Sarah – Yes. I opened it because it was too hot.

Robert – (*gulps*) Oh, no!

Act 4

Narrator – Robert closed his eyes.

Robert – It's no good. I have to do it! Sarah, you stay here. Lock the door after I have gone.

Sarah – Where are you going, Robert?

Robert – I have to lock the window in the living room. Or the wolf may come into the house.

Sarah – Be careful.

Robert – I will!

Narrator – Robert left the room. He went downstairs.

Robert – Here goes.

Narrator – He closed the window.

Robert – (*sighs*) Phew!

Wolf – (*growls*)

Robert – What?

Narrator – Robert turned. The wolf was standing right behind him.

Robert – Oh no! Don't hurt me! Dad! Dad!

Narrator – Robert took a step back. The wolf was creeping towards him.

Robert – (*in a panic*) What should I do?

Narrator – He saw a poker by the fire. He picked it up.

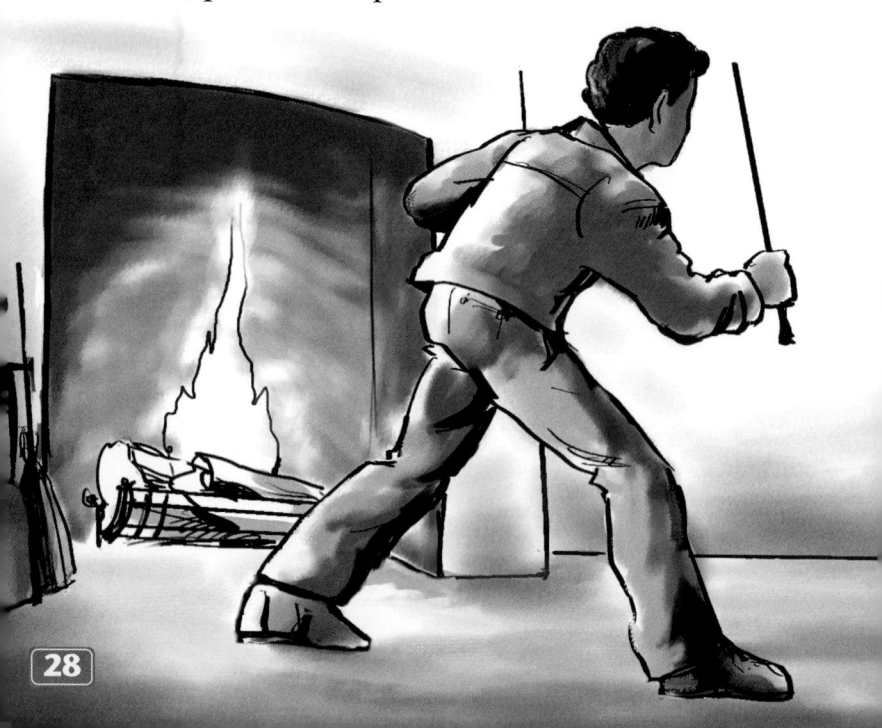

Wolf – (*growls*) Grrr… Robert!

Robert – What!

Narrator – Robert froze.

Wolf – (*howls*) No-o-o-o-o!

Narrator – Robert could not believe his eyes. A shape stood where the wolf had been.

Robert – Dad? What are you doing here? What happened to the wolf?

Dad – (*sighs*) Oh, I'm sorry about that. I didn't want to scare you.

Robert – You didn't scare me, Dad. The wolf did.

Dad – Ah. Robert, there is something I have to tell you…

Robert – What? You're a wolf? Ha! Ha!

Dad – No…

Robert – Thank goodness for that!

Dad – I'm a werewolf.

Robert – A what?

Dad – When the full moon shines I turn into a wolf. And when you grow up… you and Sarah will be the same. I'm so sorry.

Robert – Don't be sorry, Dad. Being a werewolf sounds cool!

Dad – Really? Well it can be fun, but you have to be careful not to eat anyone.

Robert – Even if you don't like them?

Dad – Yes, even if you don't like them. Now, come on. Let's go and find Sarah and make sure she's cleaned her teeth.

Robert – Why?

Dad – She's going to need them when she's a werewolf!

THE END